Our Favorite
One-Dish Dinner
Recipes

Copyright 2017, Gooseberry Patch

Bake a shortcake for dessert to fill with strawberries or peaches. Mix up 2-1/3 cups biscuit baking mix, 3 tablespoons sugar, 1/2 cup milk and 3 tablespoons melted margarine. Pat into an ungreased 9" round cake pan. Bake at 350 degrees until golden, 10 to 12 minutes. Split while still warm, layer with fruit and whipped cream and cut into wedges...mmm!

Homestyle Beef Pot Pie

Serves 6 to 8

16-oz. pkg. frozen mixed
   vegetables
2 T. water
1/2 t. dried thyme
12-oz. jar mushroom gravy

1 lb. leftover roast beef, cubed
pepper to taste
8-oz. tube refrigerated
   crescent rolls

Combine frozen vegetables, water and thyme in a skillet. Cook over
medium heat until vegetables are thawed, about 3 minutes. Stir in gravy;
bring to a boil. Remove from heat. Add beef; mix well. Transfer to an
ungreased 9" glass pie plate and sprinkle with pepper. Separate crescent
rolls into 8 triangles. Starting at wide ends, roll up halfway; arrange
over beef mixture so pointed ends are directed to the center. Bake at
375 degrees for 17 to 19 minutes, until rolls are golden. Cut into wedges
to serve.

There is nothing better on a cold wintry day
than a properly made pot pie.

–Craig Claiborne

Homemade Turkey Pot Pie

Makes 9 servings

1/3 c. margarine
1/3 c. onion, chopped
1/3 c. all-purpose flour
1/2 t. salt
1/4 t. pepper
1-3/4 c. turkey or chicken broth

2/3 c. milk
2-1/2 to 3 c. cooked turkey, chopped
10-oz. pkg. frozen peas & carrots, thawed
2 9-inch pie crusts, unbaked

Melt margarine in a large saucepan over low heat. Stir in onion, flour, salt and pepper. Cook, stirring constantly, until mixture is bubbly; remove from heat. Stir in broth and milk. Heat to boiling, stirring constantly. Boil and stir for one minute. Mix in turkey, peas and carrots; set aside. Roll out each pie crust into an 11-inch by 11-inch square. Arrange one crust in an ungreased 9"x9" baking pan. Spoon turkey mixture into pan. Place remaining crust over filling; turn edges under and crimp. Bake at 425 degrees for about 35 minutes, until crust is golden. Cut into wedges to serve.

Sun-ripened tomatoes are such a treat! Serve them up with just a dash of oil & vinegar, a pinch of salt and a toss of chopped fresh basil. When garden tomatoes aren't in season, try roma tomatoes...they're available year 'round.

Italian Chicken Pie

Serves 6 to 8

3/4 c. cottage cheese
1/3 c. grated Parmesan cheese
1-1/2 c. cooked chicken, cubed
1-1/4 c. shredded mozzarella
    cheese, divided
6-oz. can tomato paste
1/2 t. garlic powder

1/2 t. dried oregano
1/2 t. dried basil
1 c. milk
2 eggs, beaten
2/3 c. biscuit baking mix
1/4 t. pepper

Layer cottage cheese and Parmesan cheese in a greased 10" pie plate.
Combine chicken, 1/2 cup mozzarella cheese, tomato paste and
seasonings; spoon over Parmesan cheese. Beat remaining ingredients
until smooth; pour over chicken mixture. Bake, uncovered, at 400 degrees
for 30 minutes. Top with remaining mozzarella cheese. Bake 5 to
8 minutes longer, until a knife tip inserted in center comes out clean.
Cut into wedges to serve.

A sweet china saucer that has lost its teacup
makes a useful spoon rest on the stovetop.

Daddy's Shepherd's Pie

Makes 6 to 8 servings

1 lb. ground beef
10-3/4 oz. can cream of
    mushroom soup
2/3 c. water
7.2-oz. pkg. homestyle creamy
    butter-flavored instant
    mashed potato flakes

2 c. corn
8-oz. pkg. shredded Cheddar
    cheese

Brown beef in a skillet over medium heat; drain. Stir in soup and water; simmer until heated through. Meanwhile, prepare potato flakes as package directs; set aside. Transfer beef mixture to a 13"x9" baking pan sprayed with non-stick vegetable spray. Top with corn; spread potatoes evenly across top. Sprinkle with cheese. Bake, uncovered, at 425 degrees for about 10 minutes, until hot and cheese is melted. Cut into squares to serve.

Shake up some fresh herbed vinaigrette dressing. In a jar, combine 3/4 cup olive oil, 1/4 cup white wine vinegar, 1/4 cup fresh basil, 1/4 cup fresh parsley and a tablespoon of sliced green onions. Shake well and toss with salad greens.

Stacie's Spaghetti Pie

Makes 6 to 8 servings

8-oz. pkg. spaghetti, cooked
2 t. olive oil
1 c. favorite pasta sauce
1 c. sliced mushrooms
1/2 c. green pepper, chopped
1/2 c. black olives, chopped
1/4 lb. mozzarella cheese, cubed
2 t. garlic, minced

1/2 t. Italian seasoning
1/2 t. seasoning salt
1/4 t. red pepper flakes
4 eggs, beaten
1/2 c. milk
3/4 c. sliced pepperoni
1/2 c. grated Parmesan cheese

Toss cooked spaghetti with oil in a large bowl. Add sauce, vegetables,
mozzarella cheese, garlic and seasonings. Mix well; spread in a lightly
greased 13"x9" baking pan. Whisk together eggs and milk; pour over
spaghetti mixture. Arrange pepperoni evenly on top; sprinkle with
Parmesan cheese. Bake, uncovered, at 375 degrees for 25 to 30 minutes,
until bubbly and golden. Let stand for 5 minutes; cut into squares
to serve.

A dollop of homemade guacamole jazzes up any south-of-the-border meal. Slice a couple of ripe avocados, scoop them into a bowl and mash with a fork to the desired consistency. Stir in 1/2 cup of your favorite salsa, a teaspoon of lime or lemon juice and a dash of salt...yum!

Mexicalli Pie

1 lb. ground beef
1/2 c. onion, chopped
1/2 c. green pepper, chopped
1-1/2 c. frozen corn, thawed
  and drained
1 c. chunky-style zesty salsa
3/4 c. shredded sharp or Mexican-
  style Cheddar cheese

1/8 t. pepper
1 c. corn chips, crushed
Garnish: sour cream,
  sliced jalapeño peppers,
  diced tomato

Brown beef, onion and green pepper in a skillet over medium heat; drain.
Add corn, salsa, Cheddar cheese and pepper. Spoon beef mixture into a
lightly greased 10" pie plate; top with crushed chips. Bake, uncovered, at
350 degrees for 30 minutes. Let cool for 10 minutes; cut into wedges to
serve. Garnish as desired.

Get the day off to a great start...put together a breakfast quiche or casserole and refrigerate. The next day, pop it in the oven for a hot, hearty breakfast with no fuss at all!

Farm-Fresh Spinach Quiche

Serves 4 to 6

9-inch pie crust, unbaked
8 slices bacon, crisply cooked
    and crumbled
8-oz. pkg. shredded Monterey
    Jack cheese

3 eggs, beaten
1-1/2 c. milk
1 T. all-purpose flour
10-oz. pkg. frozen spinach,
    thawed and drained

Lay pie crust in an ungreased 9" pie plate. Sprinkle half of crumbled bacon into pie crust; set aside. Mix together cheese, eggs, milk, flour and spinach; spoon into crust. Sprinkle remaining bacon on top. Bake, uncovered, at 350 degrees for one hour, or until center is set. Cut into wedges to serve.

The simplest way to plan a party...choose a theme! Whether it's Fiesta Night, 1950's Diner or Hawaiian Luau, a theme suggests appropriate dishes, decorations and music, and gives guests something fun to look forward to.

Fiesta Taco Pie

Makes 6 to 8 servings

8-oz. tube refrigerated crescent
    rolls
1 c. nacho cheese tortilla chips,
    crushed and divided
1 lb. ground beef
1 onion, chopped
8-oz. can tomato sauce
1-1/4 oz. pkg. taco seasoning mix
3 T. sour cream
1 c. shredded Cheddar cheese

Separate crescent rolls and line an ungreased 9" pie plate with them;
press together to form a pie crust. Sprinkle with 1/3 cup crushed tortilla
chips; set aside. Brown beef and onion in a skillet over medium heat;
drain. Stir in tomato sauce and taco seasoning; simmer for 5 minutes.
Spoon beef mixture into pie crust. Spread sour cream over top; sprinkle
with cheese and remaining chips. Bake, uncovered, at 350 degrees for
20 minutes. Cut into wedges to serve.

Show off the bright colors of a fruit salad
by serving it in old-fashioned glass compotes.

Pizzeria Pot Pie

Serves 6

1 lb. ground turkey sausage
1/2 c. onion, chopped
1-1/2 c. sliced mushrooms
1 c. green pepper, chopped
14-1/2 oz. can chunky
    pizza sauce

2 c. biscuit baking mix
1/4 c. milk
1 egg, beaten
2 T. grated Parmesan cheese

Brown sausage and onion in a skillet over medium heat; drain. Stir in mushrooms, pepper and pizza sauce; spoon into an ungreased 3-quart casserole dish and set aside. Stir baking mix, milk, egg and cheese together until dough forms. Turn onto a floured surface; knead 10 times. Pat dough into a 9-inch circle; cut into 6 wedges. Arrange wedges over sauce mixture. Bake, uncovered, at 400 degrees for about 30 minutes, until crust is golden. Cut into wedges to serve.

A refreshing beverage for a spicy supper! Combine equal amounts of ginger ale and pineapple juice. Pour into ice-filled tumblers and garnish with fresh fruit slices stacked up on drinking straws.

Country Ham & Potato Pie

Makes 4 to 6 servings

2 potatoes, peeled and sliced
2 c. cooked ham, cubed
1 onion, sliced
2 c. shredded Cheddar cheese
3 T. all-purpose flour
1 t. garlic salt

1/4 t. pepper
1/8 t. nutmeg
1 c. milk
1 T. margarine, diced
9-inch pie crust, unbaked
1/2 c. whipping cream

Layer potatoes, ham and onion in a lightly greased 9" round baking pan; set aside. Mix together cheese, flour and seasonings; sprinkle over ham mixture. Pour milk over the top; dot with margarine. Place pie crust on top; cut 4 slits in the center. Bake, uncovered, at 350 degrees for one hour; remove from oven. Pour cream into slits in crust; let stand for 10 minutes. Cut into wedges to serve.

A recipe for success! Always check the recipe and
make sure you have everything on hand before
you start...no quick trips to the store
for a forgotten ingredient.

Souper Meat & Potatoes Pie

Makes 4 to 6 servings

1 lb. ground beef
10-3/4 oz. can cream of
    mushroom soup, divided
1/4 c. onion, chopped
1 egg, beaten
1/4 c. dry bread crumbs
2 T. fresh parsley

1/4 t. salt
1/8 t. pepper
2 c. potatoes, peeled, cooked
    and mashed
1/4 c. shredded mild Cheddar
    cheese

Mix uncooked beef, 1/2 cup soup, onion, egg, bread crumbs, parsley and seasonings. Press firmly into an ungreased 9" pie plate. Bake, uncovered, at 350 degrees for 25 minutes; drain. Layer potatoes, remaining soup and cheese on top. Bake an additional 10 minutes. Cut into wedges to serve.

While dinner is cooking, mix up some good clean fun with homemade bubble solution! Stir together 5 cups water, 2 cups dishwashing liquid and 1/2 cup light corn syrup. Let the kids explore the kitchen for pancake turners, strainers and other utensils to use as bubble wands.

Homestyle Tuna Pot Pie

2 9-inch pie crusts, unbaked
12-1/2 oz. can tuna, drained
    and flaked
10-3/4 oz. can cream of potato
    soup

10-oz. pkg. frozen peas & carrots
1/2 c. onion, chopped
1/3 c. milk
1/2 t. dried thyme
salt and pepper to taste

Line an 8"x8" baking pan with one pie crust. Combine remaining ingredients and pour into crust; top with remaining crust. Seal and crimp the edges; make several slits in crust to vent. Bake at 375 degrees for 50 minutes, until golden. Cut into squares to serve.

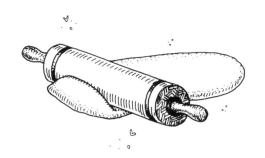

A Grandma-style treat...roll out extra pie dough, cut into strips and sprinkle with cinnamon-sugar. Bake at 350 degrees until golden, about 10 minutes.

Lattice Chicken Pot Pie

Makes 6 servings

1 to 2 boneless, skinless chicken
    breasts, cooked and cubed
4 c. frozen mixed vegetables,
    thawed
10-3/4 oz. can of cream of
    chicken soup
10-3/4 oz. can of cream of
    mushroom soup
1-1/2 t. dried rosemary
8-oz. tube refrigerated
    crescent rolls

In a large bowl, mix all ingredients except crescent rolls. Spoon into a
lightly greased 13"x9" baking pan. Roll out crescent rolls without
separating them; pinch gently to close seams. Cut dough lengthwise into
one-inch strips. Criss-cross strips over pan in a lattice pattern. Bake at
350 degrees for one to 1-1/2 hours, until bubbly and crust is golden.
Cut into squares to serve.

Bake up some sweet and tangy cranberry muffins for dinner!
Just stir dried cranberries and a little orange zest into
a cornbread muffin mix. Bake as directed on the package...
serve topped with a pat of butter. Yum!

BBQ Chicken Quiche

Makes 8 servings

4 eggs, beaten
1 c. half-and-half
1 c. barbecued chicken, cubed

1/2 c. onion, finely chopped
9-inch pie crust, unbaked

Whisk together eggs and half-and-half. Add chicken and onion; mix well. Spoon mixture into pie crust. Bake, uncovered, at 350 degrees for 40 minutes, or until bubbly and golden. Cut into wedges to serve.

After you unpack groceries, take just a little time to
prep ingredients and place them in plastic zipping bags...wash and
chop fruits and vegetables and place meats in marinades.
Weeknight dinners will be so much easier.

Oktoberfest Pie

Makes 6 servings

14-oz. pkg. Kielbasa turkey
  sausage, sliced 1/2-inch thick
14-oz. can sauerkraut, drained
1 c. shredded Swiss cheese
2 eggs, beaten

3/4 c. low-fat biscuit baking mix
1/2 c. skim milk
1/2 c. regular or non-alcoholic
  beer

Spray a 9" glass pie plate with non-stick vegetable spray. Layer Kielbasa, sauerkraut and cheese in pie plate; set aside. In a bowl, stir together remaining ingredients until well blended; pour over cheese. Bake, uncovered, at 400 degrees for about 35 minutes, until golden. Let stand several minutes. Cut into wedges to serve.

In a hurry? Use a food processor to
quickly chop potatoes and carrots.

Zucchini Quiche

Serves 4 to 6

3 c. zucchini, thinly sliced
1 c. biscuit baking mix
1/2 c. onion, chopped
1/2 c. grated Parmesan cheese
2 T. dried parsley
1/2 t. salt

1/2 t. dried oregano
1/8 t. pepper
1/8 t. garlic powder
1/2 c. oil
4 eggs, slightly beaten

Combine all ingredients in a large bowl; blend well. Spoon into a greased 9" round baking pan. Bake, uncovered, at 350 degrees for 45 minutes, or until lightly golden. Cut into wedges to serve.

Homemade applesauce goes so well with pork chops...why not make some while dinner is cooking? Peel, core and chop 4 tart apples. Combine with 1/4 cup water, 2 teaspoons brown sugar and 1/8 teaspoon cinnamon in a microwave-safe bowl. Cover and microwave on high for 8 to 10 minutes. Mash apples with a potato masher and serve warm, dusted with a little more cinnamon.

Pork Chop Skillet Supper

Makes 6 servings

1/2 c. all-purpose flour
6 bone-in pork loin chops,
    3/4-inch thick
2 T. olive oil
2 t. dried thyme
2 t. salt
1/4 t. pepper

4 to 5 potatoes, peeled and cut
    into 3/4-inch cubes
5 carrots, peeled and sliced
    1/4 inch thick
1 onion, cut into wedges
3 c. beef broth

Place flour in a large resealable plastic zipping bag. Add pork chops to bag, a few at a time; shake to coat. Heat oil in a large skillet over medium heat; brown pork chops on both sides. Drain; season with thyme, salt and pepper. Add vegetables to skillet. Pour broth into skillet; bring to a boil. Reduce heat to medium-low. Cover and simmer for 40 to 50 minutes, until pork chops are no longer pink inside and vegetables are tender.

Look for inexpensive Asian-themed plates, bowls and teacups at an import store. They'll make even the simplest Oriental meals special. Don't forget the fortune cookies!

Ramen Skillet Supper

1 lb. ground beef
2-1/2 c. water
2 3-oz. pkgs. beef-flavor ramen
    noodles with seasoning
    packets

1/2 c. stir-fry sauce
3 c. frozen stir-fry vegetables

Brown beef in a large skillet over medium heat; drain. Add water,
one seasoning packet, stir-fry sauce and vegetables; bring to a boil.
Reduce heat to medium-low. Cover and cook, stirring occasionally, for
5 minutes, or until vegetables are crisp-tender. Break up noodles; add to
skillet. Cover and cook for 5 to 8 minutes, stirring occasionally, until
sauce is thickened and noodles are tender.

There's no need to be formal with one-pot meals...
set the pot in the center of the dinner table and
let everyone help themselves!

Ham & Potato Skillet Supper

Serves 6

4-1/2 t. butter
3 baking potatoes, peeled, thinly
    sliced and divided
1/2 onion, chopped and divided
1/2 green pepper, chopped
    and divided

2 c. cooked ham, diced
    and divided
salt and pepper to taste
3 eggs, lightly beaten
1/2 c. shredded Cheddar cheese

Melt butter in a large skillet over medium heat. Layer half each of the potatoes, onion, green pepper and ham in skillet. Repeat layers; season with salt and pepper. Cover and cook for 10 to 15 minutes, until potatoes are tender. Pour eggs over potato mixture; cover and cook for 3 to 5 minutes, until eggs are almost set. Sprinkle cheese over all. Remove from heat; cover and let stand until cheese is melted. Cut into wedges to serve.

Keep browned ground beef on hand for easy meal prep.
Just crumble several pounds of beef into a baking pan and
bake at 350 degrees until browned through, stirring often.
Drain well and pack recipe-size portions in freezer bags.

Southwestern Corn Skillet

1 lb. ground beef
1/2 c. onion, chopped
26-oz. jar pasta sauce
11-oz. can sweet corn &
    diced peppers

1/2 t. salt
8-oz. pkg rotini pasta, cooked
1 c. shredded Cheddar cheese
4 green onions, sliced

Brown beef and onion in a skillet over medium heat; drain. Stir in pasta sauce, corn, salt and cooked pasta. Cook and stir until heated through. Remove from heat and sprinkle with cheese. Cover and let stand until cheese is melted; sprinkle with green onions.

Upside-down pineapple cupcakes are an unexpected treat! Place a tablespoon of crushed pineapple into greased muffin cups and top with a teaspoonful of brown sugar and melted butter. Fill cups halfway with yellow cake mix batter and bake according to package directions. Turn out of cups to serve.

Chicken & Snow Pea Stir-Fry

Makes 3 to 4 servings

1 T. reduced-sodium soy sauce
1 t. chili-garlic or curry sauce
1 T. rice vinegar
2 t. toasted sesame oil
1/2 lb. boneless, skinless chicken breast, cubed
1 T. fresh ginger, peeled and minced

3 c. snow peas, trimmed
3 green onions, chopped
3 T. unsalted cashews, broken
cooked rice
Optional: additional chili-garlic sauce

Combine sauces and vinegar in a small bowl; set aside. Heat oil in a skillet over medium-high heat. Add chicken; cook and stir until no longer pink in the center. Add ginger; cook and stir for about 30 seconds. Add snow peas and onions; cook until snow peas are just tender, about 2 to 4 minutes. Add soy sauce mixture; stir to coat well. Stir in cashews just before serving. Serve over cooked rice; top with more chili-garlic sauce, if desired.

An old cast-iron skillet is wonderful for cooking up homestyle dinners. If it hasn't been used in awhile, season it first. Rub it lightly with oil, bake at 300 degrees for an hour and let it cool completely in the oven. Now it's ready for many more years of good cooking!

Western Round-Up

1 lb. ground beef
2 red peppers, cut into 2-inch
    squares
1/4 c. onion, chopped
15-oz. can baked beans

1 T. fajita seasoning mix
8-1/2 oz. pkg. cornbread mix
1 egg, beaten
1/3 c. milk

Combine beef, red peppers and onion in a large oven-safe skillet over medium-high heat. Cook and stir until beef is browned and onion is translucent; drain. Stir in beans and fajita seasoning; heat through, stirring frequently. Spread out mixture evenly in skillet; remove from heat and set aside. Prepare cornbread mix with egg and milk according to package directions. Spread batter evenly over beef mixture in skillet; place skillet in the oven. Bake, uncovered, at 350 degrees for 20 minutes, or until a toothpick inserted into cornbread layer comes out clean. Let cool slightly before serving; cut into wedges.

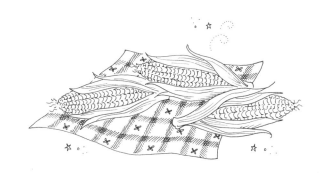

Corn on the cob is a great side that goes well with
so many quick one-dish meals. Use spray butter or
margarine...so easy and less mess!

Quick & Easy Skillet Supper

Serves 4 to 6

1-1/2 lbs. ground pork sausage
1 onion, chopped
1/4 t. pepper
1 t. dried marjoram
2 15-oz. cans diced tomatoes

10-oz. pkg. frozen chopped
   spinach, thawed and drained
5 to 6 c. cooked rotini pasta
Garnish: grated Parmesan cheese

Brown sausage in a large skillet over medium heat; drain. Add onion; sauté until tender. Stir in seasonings, tomatoes with juice and spinach; heat through. Add cooked pasta; stir gently to combine. Sprinkle with Parmesan cheese at serving time.

Serve homemade crispy tortilla chips with your Mexican-inspired dinner! Simply cut corn tortillas into wedges, spritz with non-stick vegetable spray and arrange on a baking sheet. Sprinkle with salt and bake at 350 degrees until crisp, 5 to 10 minutes. Try seasoned salt or garlic salt for an extra kick.

Taco Supper in a Skillet

Serves 4 to 6

1 lb. lean ground beef
1 onion, chopped
16-oz. can refried beans
4-oz. can chopped green chiles
1/4 to 1/2 t. garlic powder
1/2 to 1 t. chili powder
1/2 to 1 t. ground cumin
3/4 c. sour cream

8-oz. pkg. tortilla chips
1 tomato, chopped
1 green pepper, chopped
2-1/4 oz. can sliced black olives, drained
8-oz. pkg. shredded Mexican-blend cheese
Garnish: shredded lettuce, salsa

Brown beef and onion in a skillet over medium heat; drain. Stir in beans, chiles and garlic powder; heat through. Combine chili powder and cumin; sprinkle over beef mixture. Sour cream may be stirred in at this point, or may be served separately as a topping. To serve, spoon beef mixture over tortilla chips. Top with remaining ingredients.

Large bottles of olive oil stay freshest when kept in
the refrigerator. Pour a little into a small squeeze bottle
to keep in the cupboard for everyday use.

Summer Penne Pasta

Serves 4

2 T. olive oil
1 to 2 cloves garlic, pressed
2 c. broccoli flowerets
1 carrot, peeled and cut into
    thin strips
2 c. vegetable broth
8-oz. pkg. penne pasta, uncooked
1/2 t. lemon juice
salt and pepper to taste
1/2 c. grated Parmesan cheese

Heat oil in a deep cast-iron skillet over medium heat. Sauté garlic just until golden. With a slotted spoon, remove garlic from skillet, reserving oil. Add broccoli and carrot to skillet and cook 2 minutes, just until heated through. In a separate saucepan or microwave, bring vegetable broth to a boil; add to skillet. Stir in uncooked pasta and reserved garlic. Cook for 5 minutes, or until pasta is almost tender. Cover; continue cooking over medium heat for 10 minutes, or until pasta and vegetables are tender. Sprinkle in lemon juice, salt and pepper. Toss with Parmesan cheese; serve warm.

Give frozen ready-to-bake dinner rolls a homemade touch.
Before baking, brush rolls with egg beaten with a little water.
Sprinkle with sesame seed or coarse salt and bake as usual.

Speedy Chicken Cacciatore

Serves 4

4 boneless, skinless chicken
   breasts
2 T. olive oil
1 c. sliced mushrooms
Optional: 1 c. green pepper,
   sliced

14-1/2 oz. can diced tomatoes
6-oz. can tomato paste with basil,
   garlic and oregano
2/3 c. water
salt and pepper to taste
Optional: cooked angel hair pasta

In a skillet over medium-high heat, cook chicken in oil until golden, about 3 to 4 minutes per side. Remove chicken from skillet; set aside. Add mushrooms and green pepper, if using, to skillet. Cook, stirring occasionally, until tender, about 4 minutes. Stir in tomatoes with juice, tomato paste and water. Add salt and pepper as desired. Return chicken to skillet; spoon sauce over chicken. Cover and simmer until chicken juices run clear, about 15 minutes. If desired, serve with cooked angel hair pasta.

Serve slices of warm Italian bread with dipping oil as
a great side with Chicken-Sausage Skilletini. Pour a thin layer
of extra-virgin olive oil into saucers, drizzle with a little balsamic
vinegar and sprinkle with dried oregano. Scrumptious!

Chicken-Sausage Skilletini

Serves 4

1/4 c. olive oil
2 boneless, skinless chicken
    breasts, cubed
1/2 lb. spicy ground pork sausage
1 red onion, thinly sliced
2 cloves garlic, minced
14-1/2 oz. can diced tomatoes
1 red pepper, sliced

3 T. brown sugar, packed
1 t. dried basil
1/2 t. dried oregano
1/8 t. salt
1/8 t. pepper
16-oz. pkg. linguine pasta,
    cooked

Heat oil in a large skillet over medium heat. Add chicken, sausage, onion and garlic; cook until meats are browned. Drain; add remaining ingredients except pasta and simmer for 5 minutes. Add cooked pasta to skillet and mix all ingredients together. Simmer another 5 minutes, until pasta is heated through.

Egg dishes are a perfect way to use up tasty tidbits from the fridge...ham, deli meats, chopped veggies and cheese. Warm briefly in a skillet and set aside for an omelet filling or scramble the eggs right in.

Jansen Family Hash

Serves 4 to 6

2 T. butter
16-oz. pkg. hot dogs, cut
   into bite-size pieces
1 onion, chopped

6 potatoes, peeled and cubed
1/4 to 1/2 c. water
salt and pepper to taste
2 to 3 T. catsup

Melt butter in a large cast-iron skillet over medium heat. Add hot dogs
and onion; cook until hot dogs are browned and onion is translucent. Stir
in potatoes and water; season with salt and pepper. Cover and cook for
10 to 15 minutes, until potatoes are tender. Add catsup; stir well to form
a sauce and heat through.

A basket filled with different kinds of rolls and
loaves of French bread is a simple and
tasty centerpiece for a pasta dinner.

Easy Skillet Lasagna

Serves 4

1 lb. ground beef
1-1/2 T. olive oil
1/2 green pepper, finely chopped
1 onion, finely chopped
1 clove garlic, minced
16-oz. jar spaghetti sauce
6 lasagna noodles, cooked, cut in
   half and divided

12-oz. container small-curd
   cottage cheese, divided
4 slices mozzarella cheese,
   divided
1/2 c. grated Parmesan cheese,
   divided

Brown beef in a skillet over medium heat; drain and set aside beef. Add oil to skillet. Sauté green pepper, onion and garlic until tender; drain. Transfer vegetable mixture to a bowl; stir in spaghetti sauce and browned beef. In same skillet, layer 1/3 of sauce mixture, half the cooked lasagna noodles, half the cottage cheese, 2 slices of mozzarella cheese and 1/4 cup Parmesan cheese. Repeat layers. Top with remaining sauce, making sure to cover all the noodles. Cover and simmer over medium-low heat for 10 to 15 minutes. Remove from heat; let stand for 10 minutes before uncovering and serving.

To clean a cast-iron skillet, simply scrub with coarse salt,
wipe with a soft sponge, rinse and pat dry. Salt cleans cast
iron thoroughly without damaging the seasoning
as dish detergent would.

Cheesy Tuna Skillet

Serves 6

14-oz. can chicken broth
1-3/4 c. water
16-oz. pkg. rotini pasta,
    uncooked
10-3/4 oz. can of mushroom soup
1 c. milk

2.6-oz. pkg. chunk light tuna,
    flaked
1 c. shredded Cheddar cheese
1 c. shredded mozzarella cheese
1/2 c. seasoned dry bread crumbs
2 T. butter, melted

In a large non-stick skillet, bring broth and water to a boil; stir in pasta.
Return to a boil and cook for 6 to 7 minutes; do not drain. Stir in soup,
milk and tuna. Reduce heat to medium-low. Cover and cook, stirring
frequently, until pasta is tender, adding a little more milk if needed. Stir in
cheeses; cook until melted. In a small bowl, mix together bread crumbs
and butter; sprinkle over pasta mixture and serve.

For a refreshing, healthy beverage, ice-cold tea can't be beat!
Fill up a 2-quart pitcher with water and drop in 6 to 8 of your
favorite tea bags. Refrigerate overnight. Discard tea bags
and add sugar to taste; serve over ice.

Country Pork Skillet

Serves 4

4 boneless pork chops, diced
1 T. oil
12-oz. jar pork gravy

2 T. catsup
8 new redskin potatoes, diced
2 c. frozen mixed vegetables

In a skillet over medium heat, brown pork in oil; drain. Stir in gravy, catsup and potatoes; cover and simmer for 10 minutes. Stir in frozen vegetables; cook an additional 10 to 15 minutes, until vegetables are tender.

Often, casserole recipes call for precooked chicken, ham or roast beef. For a handy recipe shortcut, stop at the deli counter and order thick-sliced meat...it's ready to cube or chop as needed.

Saucy Chicken & Rice

10-3/4 oz. can cream of
  mushroom soup
10-3/4 oz. can cream of
  chicken soup
10-3/4 oz. can cream of
  celery soup

2 c. water
1-3/4 c. quick-cooking rice,
  uncooked
1-1/2 oz. pkg. onion soup mix
6 boneless, skinless chicken
  breasts

Whisk together soups and water in a bowl; stir in uncooked rice and soup mix. Transfer mixture to an ungreased 13"x9" baking pan. Gently push chicken breasts into the mixture until they are partly covered. Cover and bake at 350 degrees for 1-1/2 hours. Uncover and bake an additional 30 minutes.

Don't like broccoli? Try a package of your
favorite frozen veggies!

Chicken Comfort Casserole

Serves 6 to 8

10-3/4 oz. can Cheddar cheese
    soup
10-3/4 oz. can cream of chicken
    soup
1/2 c. chicken broth
1 c. quick-cooking rice, uncooked
4 c. cooked chicken, chopped

16-oz. pkg. frozen chopped
    broccoli, thawed
1/2 c. milk
1/4 c. butter, sliced
1/2 c. onion, chopped
salt and pepper to taste
1 c. shredded Cheddar cheese

In a large bowl, whisk together soups and broth. Stir in uncooked rice, chicken and broccoli. Stir in milk, butter and onion. Mixture will be thick. Season with salt and pepper. Spread in an ungreased 11"x7" baking pan; sprinkle with cheese. Bake, covered, at 350 degrees for 30 minutes. Uncover and bake an additional 10 minutes, until hot and bubbly. Let stand 10 minutes before serving.

While the casserole bakes, steam fresh broccoli, green beans
or zucchini in the microwave. Place cut-up veggies in a
microwave-safe container and add a little water. Cover with
plastic wrap, venting with a knife tip. Microwave on high for
2 to 5 minutes, checking for tenderness after each minute.
Uncover carefully to allow hot steam to escape.

Parmesan Potatoes & Ham

Serves 6

10-3/4 oz. can cream of
  celery soup
1/2 c. milk
pepper to taste

2 potatoes, peeled and sliced
1 onion, sliced
2 c. cooked ham, diced
2 T. grated Parmesan cheese

Stir together soup, milk and pepper in an ungreased 8"x8" baking pan.
Layer potatoes, onion and ham over soup mixture. Bake, covered, at
375 degrees for one hour. Sprinkle with cheese. Bake, uncovered, for an
additional 20 minutes, until bubbly.

While dinner simmers, pop some Parmesan bread in the oven.
Split an Italian loaf lengthwise and place on a broiler pan. Spread
with a mixture of 1/4 cup butter, 2 tablespoons grated Parmesan
cheese, 2 teaspoons minced garlic and 1/4 teaspoon oregano.
Broil until golden...scrumptious!

Grandma's Dinner Dish

1 lb. ground beef
1 onion, diced
salt and pepper to taste

14-3/4 oz. can creamed corn
2 c. mashed potatoes
1/4 c. butter, diced

Brown beef and onion in a skillet over medium heat; drain. Season with salt and pepper. Spread beef mixture in a lightly greased one-quart casserole dish; spoon creamed corn over beef. Top with mashed potatoes; dot with butter. Bake, uncovered, at 350 degrees for 45 minutes. Turn oven to broil; broil until potatoes are golden.

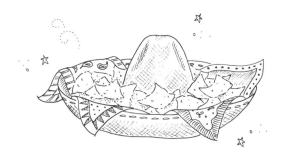

Do the unexpected at dinnertime! Line a sombrero with bandannas and fill with tortilla chips...perfect for munching while waiting for Tamale Pie to bake.

Tamale Pie

Makes 6 to 8 servings

1 onion, chopped
1 clove garlic, minced
1 T. oil
1-1/2 lbs. ground beef
15-1/4 oz. can corn, drained
14-3/4 oz. can creamed corn
4-oz. can black olives, drained
    and chopped

2 8-oz. cans tomato sauce,
    divided
2 T. chili powder
1/8 t. cayenne pepper
8-oz. pkg. corn chips, crushed

In a skillet over medium heat, sauté onion and garlic in oil just until soft.
Add beef and cook until beef loses its pink color; drain. Stir in corn,
creamed corn, olives, one can tomato sauce, seasonings and corn chips.
Transfer mixture to an ungreased 13"x9" baking pan. Top with remaining
tomato sauce. Cover and bake 45 minutes at 350 degrees.

Prefer a meatless dinner salad? Substitute roasted, salted pecans for crispy bacon as a salad topping with a similar salty-smoky taste and crunch.

Green Bean, Ham & Potato Bake

Serves 6

1 onion, chopped
2 cloves garlic, minced
1 T. butter
3 potatoes, diced
salt and pepper to taste

2 14-1/2 oz. cans green beans,
   drained
1-1/2 c. cooked ham, cubed
2 sprigs fresh rosemary, chopped
1 c. water

In a skillet over medium-high heat, sauté onion and garlic in butter. Add potatoes, salt and pepper; cook until potatoes are crisp. In a greased 13"x9" baking pan, combine potato mixture, green beans, ham and rosemary. Drizzle water over all. Cover with aluminum foil and bake at 350 degrees for one hour, or until potatoes are tender.

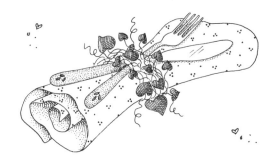

Whether dinner is casual, served in the kitchen, or a little more formal at the dining table, be sure to add simple, special touches...colorful napkins tied in a knot or perky blossoms tucked into a canning jar make mealtime more fun!

Pot Roast Casserole

Serves 4

8-oz. pkg. fine egg noodles,
    cooked
2 c. leftover roast beef, cubed

2 c. Alfredo sauce
1 c. sliced mushrooms
1/4 c. soft bread crumbs

Combine cooked noodles, beef, Alfredo sauce and mushrooms in an ungreased 2-quart casserole dish. Stir gently; sprinkle with bread crumbs. Bake, uncovered, at 350 degrees for 20 to 30 minutes, until crumbs are golden.

Try this refreshing salad! Peel and thinly slice 3 cucumbers and one small red onion. Toss with 2 tablespoons chopped fresh dill and one tablespoon each lemon juice, vegetable oil and sugar. Season with 3/4 teaspoon salt and refrigerate, covered, for 2 hours.

Turkey Almond Casserole

Serves 6

2 10-3/4 oz. cans cream of
    mushroom soup
1/2 c. mayonnaise
1/2 c. sour cream
2 T. onion, chopped
2 T. lemon juice
1 t. salt
1/2 t. pepper
5 c. cooked turkey, cubed

3 c. cooked rice
4 stalks celery, chopped
8-oz. can sliced water chestnuts,
    drained
1-1/4 c. sliced almonds, divided
1-1/2 c. round buttery crackers,
    crushed
1/3 c. butter, melted

In a large bowl, combine soup, mayonnaise, sour cream, onion, lemon juice and seasonings; mix well. Stir in turkey, cooked rice, celery, water chestnuts and one cup almonds. Transfer to a greased 13"x9" baking pan; set aside. Mix remaining almonds, cracker crumbs and melted butter; sprinkle over top. Bake, uncovered, at 350 degrees for 35 to 40 minutes, until bubbly and golden.

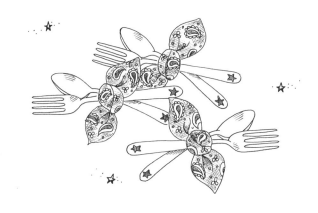

Carry out a country theme in your place settings.
Simply wrap a bright red bandanna around each set of
tableware and tie a big knot.

Cowboy Dinner

1 lb. ground beef
1/4 c. onion, chopped
1/2 c. celery, chopped
1/2 c. green pepper, chopped
15-oz. can pork & beans

1/2 c. barbecue sauce
salt and pepper to taste
11-oz. tube refrigerated
   bread sticks

Brown beef in a skillet over medium heat; drain. Add onion, celery and green pepper; cook until vegetables are crisp-tender. Stir in beans, barbecue sauce and seasonings. Transfer mixture to a greased 2-quart casserole dish. Gently unroll bread sticks; coil and lay across casserole to cover. Bake, uncovered, at 350 degrees for 20 to 25 minutes, until bubbly and bread sticks are golden.

It's so easy to double casserole recipes and freeze half for another night. When you're busy or just don't feel like cooking, you'll have a warm, yummy meal.

Perfect Cheesy Pasta Bake

Serves 4 to 6

16-oz. pkg. rotini pasta,
   uncooked
3-1/2 c. spaghetti sauce
1/2 c. grated Parmesan cheese

1 c. cooked chicken, diced
1/2 c. shredded mozzarella cheese
1/2 c. shredded pasteurized
   process cheese spread

Measure out 4 cups uncooked pasta, reserving the rest for another recipe. Cook pasta as package directs; drain and place in a large bowl. Add spaghetti sauce and Parmesan cheese; mix well. Transfer half of pasta mixture into a greased 8"x8" baking pan. Add chicken; cover with remaining pasta mixture. Top with cheeses. Bake, uncovered, at 350 degrees for 30 to 35 minutes, until hot and bubbly.

Cook up a big pot of chicken to freeze for later. For juicy, flavorful chicken, cover with water and simmer gently until cooked through, then turn off the heat and let the chicken cool in its own broth. Shred or cube chicken, wrap well in recipe-size portions and freeze.

Joyful Quilters' Chicken Casserole

Serves 8 to 10

2 c. onion, chopped
2 T. butter
10-oz. pkg. baby spinach
10-3/4 oz. can cream of
  chicken soup
2/3 c. cream of mushroom soup
2 T. chopped green chiles
10-oz. can diced tomatoes with
  green chiles

1 c. sour cream
1-1/2 t. salt
12-oz. pkg. tortilla chips, divided
4 to 6 c. cooked chicken breasts,
  cubed and divided
8-oz. pkg. shredded Monterey
  Jack cheese, divided

Sauté onion in butter in a large skillet over medium heat. Stir in spinach, soups, chiles, tomatoes with chiles, sour cream and salt. In a lightly greased 13"x9" baking pan, alternate layers of chips, chicken, spinach mixture and cheese. Repeat layers, ending with cheese. Bake, uncovered, at 350 degrees for 30 to 40 minutes, until lightly golden on top. Let stand for 5 minutes before serving.

To test for doneness, insert the tip of a table knife in the center of a casserole. If the knife tip is hot to the touch when pulled out, the casserole should be heated through. Good to know when baking a casserole that's been made ahead and stored in the fridge.

Southwest Potato Puff Bake

Serves 6 to 8

1/2 lb. ground pork sausage
1/2 c. green pepper, chopped
1/2 c. onion, chopped
30-oz. pkg. frozen shredded
   hashbrowns, thawed

1 c. shredded Cheddar cheese,
   divided
4 eggs, beaten
1/2 c. milk
Garnish: salsa

Brown sausage with pepper and onion in a skillet over medium heat; drain. Layer hashbrowns in a greased 13"x9" baking pan; top with 1/2 cup cheese and sausage mixture. Whisk together eggs and milk; pour over top. Sprinkle with remaining cheese. Bake at 350 degrees for 30 minutes. Serve garnished with salsa.

A busy-day hint...if family members will be eating at different times, spoon casserole ingredients into individual ramekins for baking. Each person can enjoy their own fresh-from-the-oven mini casserole.

Spuds & Sausages One-Dish

Makes 4 to 6 servings

4 c. boiling water
1 c. milk
1/4 c. butter, sliced
2 5-oz. pkgs. au gratin potatoes
    mix

16-oz. pkg. mini smoked
    sausages
Optional: shredded Cheddar
    cheese

Combine boiling water, milk, butter and sauce mixes from potatoes in
a greased 13"x9" baking pan; mix well. Stir in potatoes and sausages;
top with cheese, if desired. Bake, uncovered, at 400 degrees for
35 minutes, until bubbly and potatoes are tender. Let stand for
5 minutes before serving.

What a time-saver! Most casseroles can be prepared
the night before... just cover and refrigerate. Simply add
15 to 20 minutes to the original baking time.

Texas Two-Step Casserole

Serves 6 to 8

1 lb. ground turkey
1 T. olive oil
1 onion, chopped
3 cloves garlic, minced
1 red chili pepper, finely chopped
1 red pepper, chopped
1/4 c. sour cream
1 c. shredded Cheddar cheese, divided

2-1/4 oz. can sliced black olives, drained
1 T. butter, softened
1/2 t. dried parsley
1/2 t. ground cumin
salt and pepper to taste
Optional: 2 T. salsa
8-oz. pkg. rotini pasta, cooked

In a skillet over medium heat, brown turkey in oil; drain. Add onion, garlic and peppers; sauté until soft. Stir in sour cream, 1/2 cup cheese, olives, butter, seasonings and salsa, if using. Fold in cooked pasta. Transfer mixture into a greased 13"x9" baking pan. Top with remaining cheese. Bake, covered, at 350 degrees for one hour.

It's simple to make your own bread crumbs for crunchy casserole toppings. Save extra bread slices (leftover "heels" are fine) and freeze in a plastic bag. When you have enough, bake the slices in a 250-degree oven until dry and crumbly, then tear into sections and pulse in a food processor or blender.

Cajun Crab Casserole

8-oz. can crabmeat, drained
   and flaked
10-3/4 oz. can cream of
   mushroom soup
1/2 c. prepared herb-flavored
   stuffing mix

1/2 c. green pepper, diced
1/2 c. celery, diced
1/2 c. mayonnaise
hot pepper sauce and Cajun
   seasoning to taste

Combine all ingredients. in a bowl; mix well. Transfer to a greased
1-1/2 quart casserole dish. Bake, uncovered, at 350 degrees for
45 minutes to one hour, until hot and bubbly.

Crisp coleslaw is the perfect partner to fish dishes. Blend a
bag of shredded coleslaw mix with 1/2 cup mayonnaise,
2 tablespoons milk, one tablespoon vinegar and 1/2 teaspoon
sugar. For a yummy variation, toss in some mandarin oranges
or pineapple tidbits. Chill for about one hour before serving.

Updated Tuna Casserole

Serves 4 to 6

16-oz. pkg. whole-wheat rotini
    pasta, uncooked
2 5-oz. cans tuna, drained
10-oz. pkg. frozen peas, thawed
2 10-3/4 oz. cans cream of
    onion soup

1/2 c. fresh parsley, chopped
pepper to taste
1/2 c. seasoned dry bread crumbs
2 T. butter, sliced

Cook pasta according to package directions; drain and return to cooking pot. Add tuna, peas, soup, parsley and pepper; mix thoroughly. Transfer to a greased 2-quart casserole dish; top with bread crumbs and butter. Bake, uncovered, at 350 degrees for 15 to 20 minutes, until bubbly and golden.

Turn an expandable check file into a coupon organizer. Most check files have lots of tabbed pockets and an elastic-cord fastener. Personalize yours by labeling with most-used categories and decorate it with stickers or pretty paper. At the checkout counter, coupons will be right at your fingertips!

Potato-Bacon Chowder

Makes 6 servings

2 c. potatoes, peeled and cubed
1 c. onion, chopped
1 c. water
8 slices bacon
10-3/4 oz. can cream of
    chicken soup

1 c. sour cream
2 c. milk
1/2 t. salt
1/8 t. pepper

In a large saucepan over medium heat, cook potatoes and onion in water until tender, 10 to 15 minutes. Do not drain. Meanwhile, in a large skillet over medium heat, cook bacon until crisp; drain and set aside. Whisk together soup, sour cream and milk. Add soup mixture to potato mixture along with crumbled bacon, salt and pepper. Heat through over low heat; do not boil.

Wide-rimmed soup plates are perfect for serving saucy pasta dishes as well as hearty dinner portions of soup.

Tena's Delicious Gumbo

Serves 10 to 12

4 14-1/2 oz. cans chicken broth
7-oz. pkg. gumbo mix with rice
5 to 6 boneless, skinless chicken
    breasts, cooked and chopped
1 lb. Polish sausage, cut into bite-
    size pieces
2 10-oz. pkgs. frozen chopped
    okra

1 green pepper, chopped
1 red pepper, chopped
1 onion, chopped
pepper to taste
Cajun seasoning to taste
2 14-oz. pkgs. frozen popcorn
    shrimp

Combine all ingredients except shrimp in a large stockpot. Bring to a boil; reduce heat, cover and simmer for 25 minutes. Add shrimp; simmer an additional 5 to 10 minutes.

Laughter is the best dinnertime music.

-Carleton Kendrick

Chicken Tortilla Soup

Makes 10 servings

15-1/2 oz. can light red
 kidney beans
15-1/2 oz. can chili beans
15-1/2 oz. can hominy
15-oz. can corn
14-1/2 oz. can diced tomatoes
 with green chiles, or Mexican
 diced tomatoes
14-1/2 oz. can petite diced
 tomatoes
1-1/4 oz. pkg. taco seasoning mix

1-oz. pkg. ranch salad dressing
 mix
2 boneless, skinless chicken
 breasts, cooked and shredded,
 or 10-oz. can chicken, flaked
1 green onion, diced
3/4 t. garlic, minced
catsup to taste
Garnish: tortilla chips, favorite
 shredded cheese

In a large soup pot over medium heat, combine all canned vegetables
without draining. Add remaining ingredients except garnish; mix well.
Bring to a boil. Reduce heat to low and simmer, stirring often, for about
30 minutes. May also be prepared in a 6-quart slow cooker; cover and
cook on low setting for 4 to 5 hours. At serving time, ladle into soup
bowls; crumble tortilla chips over top and sprinkle with cheese.

Convert your favorite stovetop soup recipe to fix & forget in a slow cooker. Most soups that simmer for one to 2 hours will be done in 8 to 10 hours on low or 4 to 5 hours on high. Wait until the last 30 minutes to add dairy ingredients like sour cream and tender veggies like peas.

Chill-Chaser Pork Stew

Serves 6

2 to 2-1/2 lbs. pork steaks, cubed
2 T. olive oil
2 sweet onions, chopped
2 green peppers, chopped
2 cloves garlic, minced

salt and pepper to taste
6-oz. can tomato paste
28-oz. can diced tomatoes
2 8-oz. cans sliced mushrooms,
    drained

In a Dutch oven over medium heat, sauté pork in oil until browned. Add onions, green peppers, garlic, salt and pepper. Cover; cook over medium heat until pork is tender. Add tomato paste, tomatoes with juice and mushrooms; bring to a boil. Reduce heat to low; simmer for one hour, stirring often.

Keep most-used recipes at your fingertips! Tack them to
self-stick cork tiles placed inside a kitchen cabinet door.

Chicken & Dumplin' Soup

Serves 4 to 6

10-3/4 oz. can cream of
    chicken soup
4 c. chicken broth
4 boneless, skinless chicken
    breasts, cooked and shredded

2 15-oz. cans mixed vegetables
2 12-oz. tubes refrigerated
    biscuits, quartered

Bring soup and broth to a slow boil in a saucepan over medium heat; whisk until smooth. Stir in chicken and vegetables; bring to a boil. Drop biscuit quarters into soup; cover and simmer for 15 minutes. Remove from heat. Let stand 10 minutes before serving.

Leftover soup? Ladle single portions into freezer bags...
seal, label and freeze. Then, when you need a quick-fix
dinner, simply let family members choose a bag, transfer
soup to a microwave-safe bowl and reheat.

Colby Corn Chowder

Makes 12 to 14 servings

6 potatoes, peeled and diced
1 t. salt
1 onion, chopped
1/4 c. butter
2 14-3/4 oz. cans creamed corn

4 slices bacon, crisply cooked
  and crumbled
3 c. milk
8-oz. pkg. Colby cheese, cubed

Place potatoes in a soup pot; sprinkle with salt and cover with water.
Bring to a boil over medium heat. Cover and simmer until potatoes are
tender. Meanwhile, in a skillet over medium heat, sauté onion in butter
until tender. Stir in corn and bacon; heat through. Drain potatoes; return
to pot. Add milk and heat through over low heat. Stir in corn mixture
and cheese; stir until cheese is melted. Serve immediately.

Whimsical vintage salt & pepper shakers add a dash of
fun at mealtime. Look for them at flea markets or
thrift shops...you're sure to find some favorites.

Easy Brunswick Stew

Serves 6

1/2 c. onion, diced
1 T. oil
3 slices bacon, crisply cooked
    and crumbled
2 14-1/2 oz. cans chicken broth
8-oz. can tomato sauce

2 c. potatoes, peeled and cubed
1 c. canned lima or kidney beans
1 c. frozen corn
3 c. cooked chicken breast, diced
salt and pepper to taste

In a large stockpot over medium heat, sauté onion in oil until tender. Add bacon, chicken broth, tomato sauce and vegetables; bring to a boil over high heat. Reduce heat to a simmer; cook for 30 minutes. Stir in chicken, salt and pepper; heat through.

Hearty chowders are perfect for easy weeknight dinners.
Make them extra creamy and rich tasting...simply replace
the milk or water called for in the recipe with an equal
amount of evaporated milk.

Creamy White Chili

Serves 8

1 T. oil
1 lb. boneless, skinless chicken
    breast, cubed
1 onion, chopped
14-oz. can chicken broth
2 15-1/2 oz. cans Great Northern
    beans, drained and rinsed
2 4-oz. cans chopped green chiles
1-1/2 t. garlic powder

1 t. salt
1 t. ground cumin
1/2 t. dried oregano
8-oz. container sour cream
1/2 pt. whipping cream
Garnish: crushed corn chips,
    shredded Monterey Jack
    cheese

Heat oil in a large skillet over medium heat; add chicken and onion.
Sauté until chicken is cooked through; set aside. Combine broth, beans,
chiles and seasonings in a large soup pot over medium-high heat; bring
to a boil. Add chicken mixture; reduce heat and simmer for 30 minutes.
Add sour cream and whipping cream; mix well. Garnish individual
servings with chips and cheese.

Serve your family dinner in an unexpected place, just for fun...
a blanket in the backyard, a spread in the living room or even
on the front porch. It's quick & easy with a one-pot meal
and a delightful change from routine!

BBQ Sloppy Joe Soup

Makes 6 to 8 servings

1 lb. ground beef chuck
16-oz. can barbecue Sloppy Joe
  sauce
10-3/4 oz. can cream of
  potato soup
10-3/4 oz. can minestrone soup
1-1/4 c. water
15-oz. can light red kidney beans,
  drained and rinsed

14-1/2 oz. can green beans,
  drained
15-1/4 oz. can green peas,
  drained
15-oz. can diced tomatoes,
  drained
garlic powder and steak
  seasoning to taste
Garnish: oyster crackers

Brown beef in a large saucepan over medium heat; drain. Stir in Sloppy
Joe sauce; heat through. Add remaining ingredients except crackers;
simmer until bubbly, about 10 to 15 minutes. Serve with crackers.

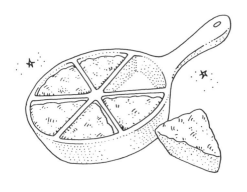

Cornbread goes well with so many quick dinners!
For cornbread with a crisp, golden crust, bake it
in a vintage sectioned cast-iron skillet.

Kielbasa Camp Stew

Makes 6 to 8 servings

1 lb. Kielbasa sausage, cut into
   1-inch slices
3 14-1/2 oz. cans diced tomatoes
2 12-oz. pkgs. frozen shoepeg
   corn
4 potatoes, peeled and diced

1/2 head cabbage, coarsely
   chopped
1 t. Cajun seasoning or other
   spicy seasoning
salt to taste

Combine Kielbasa, tomatoes with juice and remaining ingredients in a
Dutch oven; cover with water. Simmer over medium-high heat until
potatoes are tender, stirring occasionally, about 30 minutes.

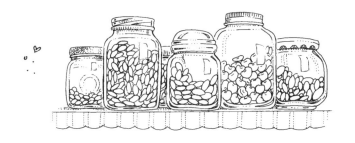

Oversized clear glass jars make attractive canisters for
storing macaroni, dried beans and rice. Because the contents
are visible, you'll always know when it's time to restock.

Fred's Chunky Chili

Serves 4 to 6

1 lb. ground beef or turkey,
    browned and drained
14-1/2 oz. can stewed tomatoes
15-1/2 oz. can kidney beans
6-oz. can tomato paste
3/4 c. green pepper, diced
3/4 c. onion, diced
1/4 c. salsa

1 t. garlic, minced
1 T. sugar
1/2 t. cayenne pepper
1/2 t. dried cilantro
1 t. dried basil
Garnish: shredded Cheddar
    cheese, crackers

Combine beef or turkey, undrained tomatoes, undrained beans and remaining ingredients except garnish in a Dutch oven. Bring to a simmer over medium-high heat. Cover and simmer over low heat for 30 minutes, stirring occasionally. Serve with cheese and crackers.

A jar of dried, minced onion can be a real timesaver!
If the recipe has a lot of liquid, such as soups and stews,
it's easy to switch. Just substitute one tablespoon of
dried, minced onion for every 1/3 cup fresh diced onion.

Farmers' Market Soup

2 c. cabbage, chopped
1 c. tomatoes, chopped
1/2 c. onion, chopped
1 c. zucchini or yellow squash,
  chopped
2 c. tomato juice
1 c. water

2 cubes beef bouillon
1 t. chili powder
1/2 t. celery seed
salt and pepper to taste
1 c. Kielbasa sausage, sliced
  and browned
1 c. thin egg noodles, cooked

In a stockpot over medium heat, combine all ingredients except sausage and noodles. Bring to a boil; reduce heat. Simmer, covered, for 45 minutes to one hour, until vegetables are tender. Add more tomato juice or water, as needed. Stir in sausage and cooked noodles; heat through before serving.

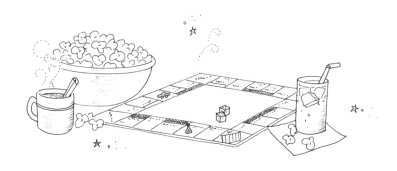

Invite family & friends over for a Game Night. After enjoying
a casual supper together, bring out all the old favorite board
games. Don't forget to supply silly prizes and big bowls of
buttered popcorn as the evening goes on!

Tastes-Like-Lasagna Soup

Makes 4 to 6 servings

1 lb. ground turkey
1/2 t. salt
seasoning salt to taste
32-oz. container chicken broth
15-oz. can tomato sauce
14-1/2 oz. can petite diced
    tomatoes

1-1/2 c. mini lasagna noodles,
    uncooked, or 4 lasagna
    noodles, uncooked and
    broken up
1/2 c. shredded mozzarella cheese
3 T. grated Parmesan cheese

Brown turkey in a large skillet over medium heat. Drain; season with salts. Add broth, tomato sauce and tomatoes with juice. Bring to a boil; reduce heat to low. Simmer, stirring occasionally, for about 20 minutes. Return to a boil; add noodles. Reduce heat to medium-low and simmer, uncovered, stirring occasionally, until noodles are tender and soup thickens slightly, 10 to 12 minutes. Remove from heat; stir in cheeses.

Dried celery leaves add homestyle flavor to soups and stews. Save the leaves from celery stalks, spread them on a baking sheet and dry slowly in a 180-degree oven for 3 hours. When they're crisp and dry, store them in a canning jar. The leaves can be crumbled right into a simmering soup pot.

Turkey Dumpling Soup

Makes 6 servings

4 c. cooked turkey, chopped
1 onion, chopped
1 green pepper, chopped
1/2 c. celery, chopped
3 c. turkey or chicken broth

salt and pepper to taste
3 c. all-purpose flour
2 t. baking powder
1/2 c. oil
1/2 c. water

In a soup pot over medium heat, combine turkey, vegetables and broth.
Bring to a boil; simmer until vegetables are tender. Season with salt and
pepper. Stir together remaining ingredients in a bowl. Add dough by
large spoonfuls to simmering soup. Cook for 8 minutes, or until
dumplings are firm.

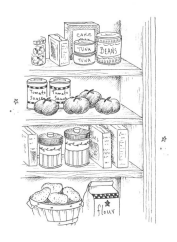

Keep the pantry stocked with canned vegetables, creamy soups, rice mixes, pasta and other handy meal-makers. If you pick up 2 or 3 items whenever they're on sale, you'll have a full pantry in no time at all.

Nana's Clam Chowder

Serves 6 to 8

3 slices bacon, diced
1 onion, diced
2 6-1/2 oz. cans chopped clams
12-oz. can evaporated milk

2 10-3/4 oz. cans cream of
  potato soup
2 T. lemon juice
1 T. pepper, or to taste

In a stockpot over medium heat, cook onion with bacon until onion is tender; drain. Stir in clams with juice and remaining ingredients. Bring to a boil; reduce heat to medium-low. Simmer for 10 to 15 minutes, stirring occasionally.

INDEX

INDEX

Our Story

Back in 1984, we were next-door neighbors raising our families in the little town of Delaware, Ohio. Two moms with small children, we were looking for a way to do what we loved and stay home with the kids too. We had always shared a love of home cooking and making memories with family & friends and so, after many a conversation over the backyard fence, **Gooseberry Patch** was born.

We put together our first catalog at our kitchen tables, enlisting the help of our loved ones wherever we could. From that very first mailing, we found an immediate connection with many of our customers and it wasn't long before we began receiving letters, photos and recipes from these new friends. In 1992, we put together our very first cookbook, compiled from hundreds of these recipes and, the rest, as they say, is history.

Hard to believe it's been over 30 years since those kitchen-table days! From that original little **Gooseberry Patch** family, we've grown to include an amazing group of creative folks who love cooking, decorating and creating as much as we do. Today, we're best known for our homestyle, family-friendly cookbooks, now recognized as national bestsellers.

One thing's for sure, we couldn't have done it without our friends all across the country. Each year, we're honored to turn thousands of your recipes into our collectible cookbooks. Our hope is that each book captures the stories and heart of all of you who have shared with us. Whether you've been with us since the beginning or are just discovering us, welcome to the **Gooseberry Patch** family!

Jo Ann & Vickie

Visit our website anytime
www.gooseberrypatch.com

Email

1·800·854·6673